DOC STULL'S

SPORTS TODAY

and IN

THE DAY

Library and Archives Cataloguing-in-Publication
Stull, Dick, 1954 –
Sports Today and in the Day/Dick Stull.
ISBN 978-1-257-03865-7

1. Stull, Dick, 1954 -   2. Sports 3. Sport History
4. Sport and Popular Culture

ACKNOWLEDGMENTS

Thanks to Danielle DeMartini for the wonderful artwork and help with the layout and design of the book.

Thanks to Michele Schiavone for her patience and editing suggestions.

Special thanks to JB Mathers who helped make my radio show Sports Today and in the Day possible, his radio colleague Tag Wotherspoon, and the folks at Bicoastal Media in Eureka.

Also thanks to Craig Riordan, Mike Angelel, Karen Price, my extraordinary musical muse Tim Randles, and, of course, most special thanks to Kathleen.

*For my son John and in memory of his
sister and my daughter, Camilla, twelve
years a champion with no peer.*

TABLE OF CONTENTS

FOREWORD

I first had the honor of meeting Doc Stull while I was a student at Humboldt State University. Doc taught one of those classes you "had" to take. It didn't take me long to understand why. Everyone should have Doc as a teacher for at least one semester in his or her life. Doc taught me about life, not how to live life but how to love life and savor every moment - the good with the bad. Life, like boxing and jazz for that matter, is never scripted, and improvisation is key.

I can't describe Doc in just a few lines, but I will say the man is an entertainer. As the radio guy that I am, that's the highest compliment I can give. It's not about being right or wrong or being an encyclopedia of knowledge, it's all about being interesting. And Doc Stull is damn good at that.

The listeners of ESPN 1340 and I are riveted and entertained for a few minutes every day when Doc brings us *Sports Today and in the Day*. If you have heard it, then you know what a treasure this book will be to read and have. For those who have not, sit back, grab a beverage of choice, and enjoy!

JB Mathers
Sports Director
ESPN 1340 AM
Eureka, California
April, 2011

Introduction

S ports *Today and in the Day* is a compendium of selected scripts from my radio shows that aired on ESPN Sports radio 1340 AM in Eureka, California in 2010 – 2011. More than sport, they're about the human condition -- they're informative, inspiring, entertaining, thought-provoking and fun. You don't have to be a sports fan to enjoy these stories.

My greatest loves since I was seven years old were sports, literature and jazz. As a young boy growing up in the Bay Area (Berkeley and Palo Alto), I was lucky to listen to great sports announcers like Russ Hodges for the San Francisco Giants, Lon Simmons for the San Francisco 49ers and Giants, and Bill King for the Oakland (Golden State) Warriors and Oakland Raiders. Their enthusiasm and word-picture painting was so captivating that often I would rather listen to them than actually see the game itself! They had their own unique delivery, their own rhythms – they were more than reporters, they were storytellers. *The San Francisco Chronicle* "in the day" had another institution, the Green Section, which was devoted to sports. My favorite sportswriter was Bob Stevens, a man who wrote with reverence, wit, soul and love – sports was always more than just a game.

Sports has drama, fun, surprise, winners, losers, personalities, the pursuit of excellence, the fall from grace, beauty, violence and you never know the script until the game is played! These themes are found in the greatest literature, too, from Homer to Shakespeare to Jack London – the quest for victory, the quest to "come home," the Aristotelian hero's reversal of fortune due to unwarranted misfortune or due to one's own pride (hubris), the search for the Holy Grail, and triumph and defeat.

Jazz, with its spontaneity on top of structure, its freedom, experimentation, rhythm, and risk, was the musical expression that most appealed to me — and I witnessed jazz in athletic performance. The three greatest athletes I ever saw--Muhammad Ali, Willie Mays and Joe Montana--were body jazz musicians playing kinetic chords in changing keys with different physical interpretations in response to events in space and time; geniuses on the playing field of sport; improvisational magicians that inspired and enthralled. Sports, great themes from literature, jazz...this is *Sports Today and in the Day*.

Dick Stull, April, 2011

Doc Stull's

Sports Today and In the Day

Jack London Calls to the Wild in Waikiki

How are you doing, everybody? This is Doc Stull for *Sports Today and in the Day*.

Surfing is now a multi-billion dollar business with high-tech boards, more than two million surfers in America alone, and worldwide thrill seekers searching out extreme waves the height of 70 feet or more. When we come back: How more than a century ago America's greatest writer of the day, Jack London, got a surfing lesson in Hawaii and helped turn America on to the sport of kings.

It's 1907, and Jack London, the American adventurer and literary superstar who wrote *The Call of the Wild*, sails with his partner Charmian from San Francisco to Hawaii. There, London is astonished to witness a small group of men walking on water along the wave breaks. Ever the sports adventurer, London manages to get introduced to a surfer of Irish and Hawaiian descent named George Freeth, one of a small set of surf riders who practiced the so-called "sport of kings," despite the native Hawaiians having been discouraged from their sacred religious sport after the arrival of missionaries to the islands. Enamored of this exotic sport and lifestyle, London published a nationwide article about his adventure in Hawaii.

The story caught the eye of a Los Angeles land speculator named Henry Huntington, who owned practically all the land in a southern California seaside town called Redondo Beach. Huntington convinced Freeth to stage surfing exhibitions at his new Hotel Redondo to attract the citizens and the money of Los Angeles to the coast. Thousands of curious Los Angelinos rode

Huntington's little red electric streetcars to see Freeth's spectacular seaside exhibitions. Freeth was surfing's resurrector and Jack London was surfing's St. Paul.

Just listen to London's majestic sports writing describing Freeth, now regarded as the Father of Modern Surfing: "His feet were buried in the churning foam, the salt smoke rising to his knees and all the rest of him in the free air and flashing sunlight. And he is flying through the air; flying forward; flying fast as the surge on which he stands. He is a Mercury. A brown Mercury. His heels are winged and in them is the swiftness of the sea." Now that's surfing sports-writing!

For *Sports Today and in the Day*, this is Doc Stull.

bruce lee
beyond east and west

How are you doing, everybody? This is Doc Stull for *Sports Today and in the Day*.

He was the son of one of the most famous actors and opera singers of his day, born of wealth and influence on his mother's side. He was a child actor, a dance champion, and by age 32 a world renowned movie actor and emerging screenwriter and director. At the time of his death, his personal library contained more than 2500 volumes, mainly in Eastern and Western philosophy. When we come back, the greatest mixed martial artist who ever lived--Bruce Lee.

A child of culture and privilege, San Francisco-born but Hong Kong-raised young Bruce Lee was a street fighter in the crowded, restless clan-riddled alleys of post–WWII Hong Kong. Lee was sent to the States by his parents to complete high school because of his rebellious nature. After finishing high school, Lee studied philosophy and theater at the University of Washington and began teaching his own eclectic fighting style, borrowing from martial arts styles ranging from wing chun to tai chi chuan to Western boxing, and accepting rival challenges from other masters and fighters to test his skills.

Later moving to Oakland, California and then Los Angeles, Lee was a physical phenom. At 5 feet 7 inches and 140 pounds, with just three percent body fat, he was capable of 50 one-armed chin-ups, bicep curls with 70 pound dumbbells, and a punching speed of five one-hundredths of a second.

In 1966 he became the first Asian-American television hero as the spin-kicking chauffeur Kato in the TV series *The Green Hornet*. His on-screen charisma and martial arts skills in *Fist of*

Fury, Way of the Dragon, and *Game of Death*, and his on-screen duels with Chuck Norris and basketball Hall of Famer Kareem Abdul-Jabbar helped his films become cinematic classics. Lee's untimely death at the age of 32 from an adverse drug reaction just days before the international release of *Enter the Dragon* in 1973 served to posthumously revolutionize the martial arts action film genre we know today.

Lee also attempted to synthesize his martial experiences and knowledge of Eastern and Western philosophy into his own treatise of fighting and living-- the Tao of Jeet Kune Do or Way of Intercepting Fist.

Bruce Lee was that rare mind, body, and spirit persona where myth, legend and reality were one and the same.

For *Sports Today and in the Day*, this is Doc Stull.

Putting Jazz on the Ball

Three Finger Mordecai Brown

How are you doing, everybody? This is Doc Stull with *Sports Today and in the Day*.

With two severely damaged fingers, gypsy jazz guitarist Django Reinhardt played solos in a way never heard before or since. What does this have to do with sports? When we come back: the tale of the young Indiana boy who had his fingers mutilated in two separate accidents at the age of five. He learned to put jazz on the ball and became the greatest Hall of Fame pitcher you've never heard of: Three Finger Mordecai Brown.

The story of Three Finger Mordecai Brown sounds like one of baseball's folktales, except it's true. Born in America's centennial year, 1876, Brown, at the age of five, had his right index finger partially severed in a farming accident and repaired by a former Civil War surgeon. Before his hand could heal, he fell and broke his fingers on the same hand, severely damaging his middle finger. Despite this, Brown proved himself to be an athlete of uncommon skill.

Starting out as a third baseman, Brown would throw to first base so hard that his throws curved unpredictably, so much so that his manager, after having dismissed his starting pitcher for showing up drunk, told Brown to take the mound. Never mind that the catcher couldn't catch him--no one could hit him. Brown eventually worked his way up to the major leagues and from 1903 to 1916 had six twenty-game seasons, won 239 games, pitched 55 shutouts, and had the fourth best ERA in major league history. Often compared to Christy Mathewson, the greatest pitcher of the era, Brown led the Cubs to the 1908 World Series Championship.

Like the great gypsy jazz guitarist Django Reinhardt, who pioneered a two-finger technique to compensate for his injured fingers, Brown used his seeming disability to put jazz on the baseball, never seen before, never seen since. And all this stuff about jazz? The word "jazz" was first used by a San Francisco sportswriter in 1912 to describe how a baseball moved unpredictably in the air, even before the term caught on to describe the last of the three most important cultural contributions by the United States to the world: the Constitution, baseball, and the music of New Orleans!

For *Sports Today and in the Day*, this is Doc Stull.

MARKETING THE MASTERS TO THE MASSES

Football and NFL Films

How are you doing, everybody? This is Doc Stull for *Sports Today and in the Day*.

What does pro football have to do with the most famous story in ancient Greece, avant-garde French film, and Hollywood movie classics? When we come back: how more than forty years ago the National Football League marketed the techniques of the world's greatest artists through the medium of television and made pro football the premier sport in America. Are you ready for some football?

The greatest marketing story rarely told is revealed in Michael Oriard's fascinating book *Brand NFL: Making and Selling America's Favorite Sport.* In the early 1960s, NFL Films' Ed Sabol and his son Steve, an art and film history major, produced NFL highlight films and football games like Hollywood movies. With melodramatic storylines drawn from Homer's epic tale of the Trojan War, creative editing montages, symphonic music, slow motion close ups, and tight narrations, NFL Films married the art masters of the past and the technology of television in a way that no other sport had done.

The Sabols borrowed images from the famous American 1946 movie western *Duel in the Sun*, so that close ups of the hands of Gregory Peck clawing his way up a hill begat the gnarled hands of offensive linemen in the trenches, breath steaming off their sweaty, dirty faces. The Sabols studied how avant-garde French filmmakers used a moving camera to tell a story within a story: the quarterback's release of a spinning spiral against a gray-scudded November sky, descending into the outstretched hands of a receiver in the corner of the end zone. The pounding music in NFL highlight films was inspired by classic film soundtracks like *The Magnificent Seven* and *Victory at Sea*. And the key to it all was the epic narration of announcer John Facenda, who in the industry was known as "The Voice of God." He told the story of the game with the power and authority of an Old Testament whirlwind.

So when you hoist a beer before the game and listen to Hank Williams Jr., tip one to the marketing visionaries of NFL films, who used the techniques of the masters to captivate the American masses. Are you ready for some football?

For *Sports Today and in the Day*, this is Doc Stull.

The Legend of Bagger Vance

Golf Meets the Gita

How are you doing, everybody? This is Doc Stull for *Sports Today and in the Day*.

The inner game of golf has captivated the imagination of players the world over ever since its 15th century origins in the windswept, seaside links-lands of Scotland. When we come back, the fascinating back story behind one of the greatest golf novels – *The Legend of Bagger Vance*, drawn from the sacred Hindu text, The Bhagavad Gītā.

One of golf's most lyrical and spiritual novels, *The Legend of Bagger Vance* relates a fictionalized golf match on a breathtaking, beautiful Krewe Island course in Savannah, Georgia in 1931. The primary characters include two American golf icons, Walter Hagen and Bobby Jones. Opposite in temperament but alike in golfing brilliance, the two champions play against a local World War I hero, Junah, a man struggling to find meaning in his life after the horrors he witnessed and suffered in war. But it's Junah's mysterious caddy, Bagger Vance, who supplies the mystical context for the story.

Unknown to many, author Steven Pressfield drew the voice of Bagger Vance from the eighteen chapters of the sacred Hindu scripture, The Bhagavad Gītā, a text that has inspired and given guidance to millions for more than six millennia. Its profound life philosophy was revered by both Mahatma Gandhi and Albert Einstein. The Bhagavad Gītā or Song of God tells of how the god Krishna gives moral advice to a young Indian prince before a great military conflict. The Gita's eighteen chapters are coded within the names of Krewe Island's eighteen holes, which appear on a map at the beginning of the novel – holes with names like vigilance, fortitude, prowess, and valor. Junah must learn the courage to face the conflict within himself, and to persevere without guarantee of success.

Junah questions the crass commercialism of the golf match and even worldly competition itself. He wants to quit, but is tasked by his caddy Bagger Vance to clear his mind of ALL but his own authentic swing.

Author Steven Pressfield's subsequent novels of ancient myth and history influenced not only legions of readers but also the leadership in the United States Armed Forces.

But it's no accident that Pressfield's literary success began with the golf novel *The Legend of Bagger Vance* and the wisdom of The Bhagavad Gītā and the message that only through conflict and struggle do we find our own authentic swing, our own authentic selves.

For *Sports Today and in the Day*, this is Doc Stull.

Hockey Hall of Famer:
Ken Dryden's The Game
Philosopher-Poet in the Goal

How are you doing, everybody? This is Doc Stull for *Sports Today and in the Day*.

He was a tall, cerebral Cornell graduate in one of the fastest, most skilled and violent games in the world - professional hockey. A goalie on the legendary Montreal Canadiens, he anchored a team that won six Stanley Cups during his eight year career. His memoir, *The Game*, is one of the great sports books of all time. When we come back, *The Game*, by a hockey player who is part poet, part philosopher and all-pro, Ken Dryden.

2003 was the 20th anniversary of one of sports finest memoirs – *The Game*, by Montreal Canadien's Hall of Fame goalie Ken Dryden. After an outstanding college career at Cornell University, he took over the goalie position with only 6 games left in his first year of professional hockey with the Montreal Canadiens in 1971. Dryden led them to the Stanley Cup championship and was the playoffs' most valuable player. The Canadiens won five more Stanley Cup Championships before he retired with a law degree in 1979 and ultimately became a member of Canada's national parliament.

Dryden ruminates on the evolution of the lines, angles and physics of the game as well as the complex psychological geometries of his teammates, the speed, athleticism and violence in the game, and the lonely mental toughness needed to play goalie facing 100 mile an hour shots on goal. He paints fascinating character sketches of pre-Gretzky hockey legends with magical names like Guy LaFleur and Bobby Orr – and the reader learns about the business of hockey which came of age in the television and expansion era of the 1970's.

But, in one of the most poetic and perceptive passages, Dryden reminisces of a different "game," about the time he played as a boy on a frozen river with miles of perfectly smooth glare ice. "The Canadian game of hockey," Dryden writes, "was weaned on long northern winters uncluttered by things to do...in long open spaces, unorganized, often solitary... it is in free time that the special player develops, not in the competitive expedience of games... but time unencumbered, unhurried, time of a different quality; to be set loose, trusted to find new instinctive directions to take, to create... Hockey has left the river and will never return.... And if the game no longer needs the place...the river is a metaphor for unorganized time alone."

For *Sports Today and in the Day*, this is Doc Stull.

Spartans and Scythians

Scintillating Women Warriors

How are you doing, everybody? This is Doc Stull for *Sports Today and in the Day.*

Tennis' Venus and Serena Williams, golf's Annika Sorenstam, and racing's Danica Patrick are but a few examples of female athletes embodying the classic ideal of swifter, higher, and stronger. It took almost three millennia to break stereotypes about the supposed inability of women to compete in sport. When we come back, the legend of the Amazons and the women of Sparta: women warrior athletes who set the standard for today's female athletes.

The Amazon myth goes back almost 3000 years, when a supposed tribe of female warriors lived in Scythia, a region near northeastern Turkey. According to legend, they cut or cauterized their right breast in order to shoot a bow or hurl a spear. A female warrior society, they had contact with men only once a year and then only to bear children. Only female babies were kept and raised. Archaeologists and historians today are finding evidence of these revered and feared female warrior tribes in antiquity.

The women of the ancient city-state of Sparta, however, required no myth. Spartan women were encouraged to wrestle, run, throw the javelin, and develop their own cunning, leadership, and self-sufficiency in the most physical and warlike culture in history. Athletic skill, strength, courage and physical beauty were expected of Spartan women. The 9th century B.C. Spartan lawgiver Lycurgus believed that for a society to be strong and healthy, so must be the women of that society, and that only strong women could raise strong men. And this was 2,800 years ago.

Today, with more and more women throughout the world participating in even the most physical and violent of sports like boxing, mixed martial arts, rugby and wrestling, it's hard to fathom that the resistance to women warriors and athletes that was the hallmark of Western society for thousands of years missed the lessons of antiquity, the myth of the Amazons, and the reality of the women of Sparta, the true forerunners of today's great female athletes. The echoes of the Amazons and the reality of the women of Sparta were etched 2000 years ago in the Roman poet Virgil's epic retelling of the Trojan War and of Camilla, the warrior queen of the Volscians:

". . . Camilla, of the Volscians bred,
  leading her mail-clad, radiant chivalry;
  a warrior-virgin . . .
  . . . bared her virgin breast
  to meet the brunt of battle, and her speed
  left even the winds behind . . . ."

For *Sports Today and in the Day*, this is Doc Stull.

Dick Fosbury: High Jumper

Desperation Plus Innovation Resets the Bar

How are you doing, everybody? This is Doc Stull for *Sports Today and in the Day*.

Almost a half century ago an awkward high school kid from Medford, Oregon revolutionized the high jump out of sheer desperation. When we come back, how Dick Fosbury's adolescent quest to not simply be average seemingly defied physics, won him an Olympic gold medal, and changed the nature of the sport.

During the 20th century a precious few individual innovations in technique truly revolutionized sport. The forward pass in football in 1913 and the jump shot in basketball in 1949 are two examples. But Dick Fosbury, a sophomore on his high school track team in the early 1960s, did not want to be mediocre. Having only limited success as a high-jumper using the then standard straddle or Western roll over the bar where you lead with your outside leg, roll your body over the bar and land on your hands and feet, Fosbury, in a moment of inspiration, innovation and desperation, and taking advantage of the newly installed foam padding in the high-jump pits, decided to go over the bar head up and backwards! To his amazement as well as his coaches', Fosbury went on to refine his run-up/approach, body position at take-off and literally draped himself backwards over the bar in what one sportswriter referred to as an "airborne seizure."

This revolutionary new style of jumping positioned his theoretical center of mass outside his body, traveling underneath the bar, according to some sport scientists, as much as eight inches. In another fascinating twist, others unknown to Fosbury and to each other had also experimented with this kind of technique including a female Canadian champion, but it was Fosbury, who later went on to study engineering and compete on the track team at Oregon State University, who refined the technique that came to be known as the "Fosbury Flop."

In 1968, Fosbury represented the United States in the Olympic Games in Mexico City and competed in a dramatic four hour jump-off for the gold medal. The enthralled, mesmerized fans in Mexico City counted in unison as Fosbury rocked to and fro before his run-up as he flopped to a gold medal and an Olympic record. Fosbury's Flop became the standard technique in high jumping – and a giant leap forward in track and field.

For *Sports Today and in the Day*, this is Doc Stull.

Ali-Frazier 1
Smoke Surrounds the Floating Butterly/Stinging Bee

How are you doing, everybody? This is Doc Stull for *Sports Today and in the Day*.

Since the recent rise of mixed martial arts, the sweet science of boxing needs to get off the deck. It's been a long time since an epic boxing match riveted the nation's and the world's attention. When we come back, the tale of two undefeated heavyweight champions, Muhammad Ali and Joe Frazier, and the supercharged cross winds of cultural change. It's Madison Square Garden, March 8, 1971-- the fight of the century.

1971: America is divided against itself over Civil Rights and the war in Vietnam. For the past three and a half years, the most charismatic heavyweight champion in history, Muhammad Ali, is banned from boxing for refusing to serve in the United States military on religious grounds. Part poet, part prophet, an athletic and verbal shape shifter, Ali floated like a butterfly and stung like a bee. But a new heavyweight champion emerged from the hot, dusty farm fields of South Carolina, via the violent gym wars of Philadelphia --proud, fearless, and ferocious Smokin'" Joe Fraizer.

Finally the courts granted Ali a license to box, and Ali v. Frazier I became the most anticipated athletic event in the world, an event where worldwide pay-per-view cable entertainment changed the face of boxing and sports forever. Ali taunted Frazier that he, Ali, was the real champion for Black Pride, the people's champion, and aroused a burning resentment deep in the lion's heart of Smokin' Joe. And on that night, it was Joe Frazier who prevailed, knocking Ali down with an exquisite left hook in the final round. Ali finished the fight, but Smokin' Joe remained undefeated. Ali tasted professional defeat for the first time. Joe Frazier would lose his title to George Foreman, never to regain it. Ali would become champion twice more and defeat Frazier in two subsequent fights, after the third of which, the Thrilla in Manila, neither fighter was ever the same.

Years after retiring, Smokin' Joe Frazier spoke at the Humboldt State University sports auction and was asked what he thought of Muhammad Ali. His response was biblical. He said, "Muhammad climbed the mountain, I climbed the ridge. Muhammad looked over me, but I was always there."

For *Sports Today and in the Day*, this is Doc Stull.

WESTWOOD WIZARD HAS THE HUMAN TOUCH

Basketball's John Wooden

How are you doing, everybody? This is Doc Stull for *Sports Today and in the Day*.

Perhaps the greatest coach ever in any sport, UCLA's basketball coach John Wooden passed away in June 2010 at the age of 99. Wooden influenced countless people beyond basketball and sport, however. More than a coach, Wooden, according to his players, family, friends, and himself, was a teacher-- a teacher of life. When we come back: the real game.

Almost 40 years ago I attended a basketball game in Palo Alto between Stanford and UCLA. Coach John Wooden's UCLA's basketball dynasty was on its way to winning seven successive NCAA championships with players like Bill Walton and Kareem Abdul-Jabbar. Their players looked like gladiators, like gods. In contrast, their white-headed bespectacled coach, holding his characteristic rolled up program in his left hand, appeared to be a high school English teacher. UCLA won the game against Stanford that night; they won them all that year.

At the final buzzer, the crowd flooded the floor to walk among the UCLA Bruins in blue and gold. I noticed a young man known to me and many of my high school buddies as Paul. Hearing-impaired since birth, he signed but never spoke. Paul was a regular seller of concessions at Stanford basketball games for as long as we could remember. He was carrying his ice cream tray, caught up amidst the throng milling around the players. I observed Coach Wooden trying to make his way to the locker room and finding himself next to Paul. Wooden reached out, tapped Paul on the shoulder, and leaned forward, appearing to speak so that Paul could lip read what he was saying. They smiled at each other for a moment and then moved off in different directions. Whether Wooden was aware that Paul was a regular at the games over the years, I have no idea, but whatever the back story, that three second moment of humanity was such a contrast to the tumult and excitement of the game. From my omniscient perch in the stands, I glimpsed the real game: how the great ones let kindness and character do the talking, even when no one seems to be watching.

For *Sports Today and in the Day*, this is Doc Stull.

The Hustler

Cruel Physics of the Green Felt

H ow are you doing, everybody? This is Doc Stull
for *Sports Today and in the Day*.

If there was ever a movie that penetrated to
the psychological bone marrow of winning, losing,
and character, it's Robert Rossen's 1961 classic, *The
Hustler*. When we come back, the game of pool
provides a backdrop for the psychological warfare
between a young hustler who thinks he can't lose,
an aging champion who's never lost, and the soulless
gambler who owns them both.

Academy Award winner Paul Newman plays a young, cocky pool hustler named "Fast Eddie" Felson, who travels cross-country to New York to challenge legendary champion Minnesota Fats. Fats, played by entertainer extraordinaire Jackie Gleason, looks as if he'll be an ex-champion after Eddie's brilliant play and dazzling shots wow the onlookers in the seedy, beshadowed pool hall that Fats owns. But Eddie's endgame disappears in a haze of booze and trash talk, and Fats' experience, poise and character combine for a championship comeback.

But the telltale heartbeat of the film is Academy Award winner George C. Scott as the sinister Bert Gordon, who brands Eddie a talented loser who could make them both rich, but at a soul-killing cost. Eddie's deal with the devil becomes the real vehicle for the film. But it's midway through the movie that Eddie captures the essence of the feeling that all athletes in any sport hunger for when he describes the game: "It's a great feeling, boy, it's a real great feeling when you're right and you know you're right. Like all of a sudden, I got oil in my arm. Pool cue's part of me. You know. . . . it's a piece of wood; it's got nerves in it. You can feel the roll of those balls. You don't have to look. You just know. You make shots that nobody's ever made before. And you play that game the way nobody's ever played it before."

Eddie's final showdown at the end of the film with Fats and Gordon combines the cruel physics of the green felt with complex twists on the themes of good and evil and how one plays the game. Made a half century ago, *The Hustler* stands as a rarified sports and life classic for the ages.

For *Sports Today and in the Day*, this is Doc Stull.

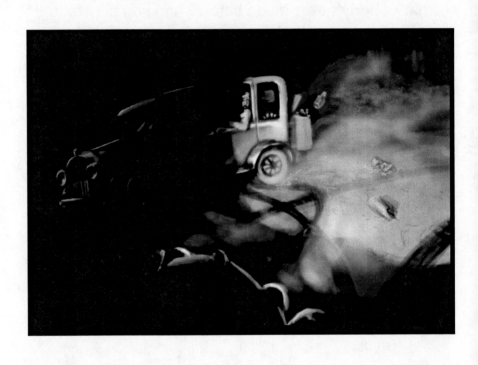

Southern Comfort on the Speed Oval

Junior Johnson

H ow are you doing, everybody? This is Doc Stull for *Sports Today and in the Day*.

Since its beginnings in 1948, NASCAR has become one of America's premier spectator sports, with driver extraordinaire Jimmie Johnson heading the field in 2010. When we come back, a look at another Johnson, Junior Johnson. His 1965 *Esquire* magazine profile, "The Last American Hero," made stock car racing and the term "good ol' boy" permanent fixtures in American popular culture.

NASCAR has come a long way since the days when its first racers honed their skills outdriving, outsmarting, and outgunning revenue agents while running moonshine, and the king of them all was Junior Johnson out of Wilkes County, North Carolina, who perfected the throw-your-car-into-second-gear, yank-the-wheel, accelerate-out-of-here, hundred-and-eighty-degree-leave-'em-in-the-dirt bootleg turn. Johnson had the Right Stuff credentials to become a NASCAR American folk hero between 1955 and 1966. No fiction writer could create a better character.

With a fiancée named Flossie, prison time wisdom, and racing against fellow good ol' boys with names like "Fireball" Roberts and Buck Baker, Johnson had cool, charisma, and three types of looks, according to writer Tom Wolfe: amiable, amiable and a little shy, and dead serious. It was Junior Johnson who epitomized stock car racing as the common man's path to freedom, a stick-it-to-the-man, anarchistic, go-for-broke, don't-tread-on-me, anti-establishment statement of independence. He represented land-bound liberation and the hot shining sun of America's new South, where even if you couldn't buy a fancy house or a big boat, you could make a statement with a fast car and live forever in those thrilling seconds during those hard left turns on the track. New breed drivers and high tech cars and another Johnson, named Jimmie, would take NASCAR into a new era in America's love affair with speed.

But America loves its nostalgia for its last American hero, as Tom Wolfe wrote about Junior Johnson almost fifty years ago: "Good old boys would wake up in the middle of the night in the apple shacks and hear an overcharged engine roaring over Brushy Mountain and say, 'Listen at him--there he goes!'"

For *Sports Today and in the Day*, this is Doc Stull.

Droids and Drugs in Sport's Brave New World

How are you doing, everybody? This is Doc Stull for *Sports Today and in the Day*.

The use of performance-enhancing drugs by some of today's superstar athletes, the revolution in the design of artificial limbs, and new exo-skeletal robotics capabilities have transformed the athlete and the world of sport. When we come back, drugs, droids, the athlete of the future and the most powerful prescription potion known to humankind since Adam took that first bite out of the apple.

When German scientists developed synthetic testosterone during the 1930s, the alchemy of peak performance became a revolutionary science. Muscle growth and strength could be chemically enhanced through anabolic steroids. The state-run regimes of the Soviet Union and the German Democratic Republic in the 1950s and 1960s systematically applied performance-enhancing drugs in their training regimens, and world records fell. More than half a century later, countries and corporations are developing new designer steroids, human growth hormone and EPO for strength and endurance, and in the United States, superstar athletes like Marion Jones in track and field, Bill Romanowski in football, Alex Rodriguez in baseball, and Floyd Landis in cycling are merely self-admitted symptoms in this brave new world that worships at the chemical altar of swifter, higher and stronger.

This is only the beginning. Gene-therapy experiments and studies at the University of Pennsylvania and National Institutes of Health give us news of "mighty-mice" with buns of steel and buffed up "bully-whippet" dogs. Couple this with new robot technologies, designer limbs, and exo-skeleton design, and the future....is now.

Fifty years ago one of television's most imaginative science fiction shows, *The Twilight Zone*, revealed our future. Boxing is banned and replaced with androids – who sock it out in the ring. A desperate android owner in need of a paycheck decides to box and enter the ring himself. He goes the distance but pays a terrible price. This may be a metaphor for our own war within ourselves. We want to be self-created gods, yet the tempting potions of power, greed and glory can burn the wings of our arrogance when we fly too close to the sun.

It all started when we took that bite out of the apple; when Prometheus stole fire from Zeus. It is our lot in sports and in life – the competition within ourselves to be gods, and be human, too.

For *Sports Today and in the Day*, this is Doc Stull.

Affirmed vs. Alydar

Triple Crown Tenacity

How are you doing, everybody? This is Doc Stull for *Sports Today and in the Day*.

The 2010 Disney movie *Secretariat* and worldwide interest in celebrity super filly Zenyatta introduced horse racing to fans who never before appreciated the sport. When we come back: The greatest horse racing rivalry ever, the Ali-Frazier of horse racing. It's 1978 and it's Affirmed versus Alydar in three wire-to-wire finishes for the Triple Crown.

---

f there was ever a horse with the heart of a champion, it was Affirmed. Not as big as Secretariat or as physically regal, Affirmed knew one thing: how to win. The great-great-grandson of War Admiral and great-great-great-grandson of Man o' War, Affirmed had a championship bloodline. Enter Alydar, a huge, beautiful come-from-behind finisher, and the table was set for a Triple Crown showdown for the ages. Affirmed beat the field and the hard charging finish of Alydar in the Kentucky Derby; Affirmed then won the Preakness, with Alydar once again just a nose behind.

And now the sports world awaited the test of champions, the longest of the Triple Crown Races at a mile and a half, the Belmont Stakes. Riding Affirmed was 17 year-old wunderkind Steve Cauthen; on Alydar, Jorge Velasquez. Alydar's owner had the blinkers removed from the horse's eyes so he could see Affirmed in this showdown. Affirmed seized the early lead but Velasquez put Alydar alongside. Now, with half a race to go, the two pulled away from the field. As Chic Anderson memorably called it:

"The pace is increasing as they come to the head of the stretch. It's still Affirmed as they come to the quarter pole. He's holding on to a head lead. Alydar is outside of him and challenging that lead. The two are heads apart. Alydar's got a lead! Alydar put a head right in front of the middle of the stretch. It's Alydar and Affirmed battling back along the inside. We'll test these two to the wire! Affirmed under a left-hand whip! Alydar on the outside driving! Affirmed and Alydar heads apart. Affirmed's got a nose in front as they come down to the wire at the finish! It's going to be dead tight. It's Affirmed!"

Only 11 horses since 1875 have won the Triple Crown. Affirmed was the last and Alydar was always there, just a nose behind.

For *Sports Today and in the Day*, this is Doc Stull.

Unseen Eyes in the Sky

Amazing Grace on the Gridiron

How are you doing, everybody? This is Doc Stull for *Sports Today and in the Day*. Sports has always had its share of classic, heart-stirring stories -- legendary Notre Dame football coach Knute Rockne's appeal to "Win One for the Gipper," and terminally ill baseball great Lou Gehrig telling 60,00 fans in Yankee Stadium that he was "the luckiest man on the face of the earth." When we come back, another story for the ages that transcends winning and losing.

A classic story often told by Columbia football coach Lou Little almost half a century ago involved a player who rode the bench for four straight years on the football team. Never good enough to start, much less even play, he was nonetheless an inspiration to his more gifted peers. He was never late to practice, gave a hundred percent, and never complained. The week before the final game in his senior year he received a telegram: his father was very ill.   His coach told him he could take the week off. But the kid practiced as usual. During the 4th quarter of the final game, he asked the coach to put him in.   With the score tied and under a minute to go in the game, the coach put him on the kick-return team. Fielding the kick at the ten yard line, he cut sharply to his left, shed two tacklers and bolted down the sideline, cut back against the grain while eluding three more defenders, and dragged two tacklers into the end zone for a score. Mobbed by his teammates in the end zone, he returned to the sidelines where his amazed coach threw his arms around the kid, and asked, "Son, what got into you? I had no idea you could play like that."

The kid lowered his head and said, "Coach, I learned just this morning that my father didn't make it. He passed away late last night. For four years he came to every one of my games and was there for me even though I never played. What you didn't know, coach, was that my father was blind, and today was the first day he ever saw me play."

For *Sports Today and in the Day*, this is Doc Stull.